Starspin

Grahaeme Barrasford Young

Stairwell Books
///

Published by Stairwell Books
161 Lowther Street
York, YO31 7LZ

www.stairwellbooks.co.uk
@stairwellbooks

Starspin © 2021 Grahaeme Barrasford Young and Stairwell Books

All rights reserved. No part of this publication may be reproduced, stored in or introduced into a retrieval system, or transmitted, in any form, or by any means (electronic, mechanical, photocopying, recording, e-book or otherwise) without the prior written permission of the author.

The moral rights of the author have been asserted.

ISBN: 978-1-913432-12-6

Layout design: Alan Gillott

Acknowledgements

Poems in this collection have appeared in:

Carillon   Dream Catcher   Envoi   Labrys
Lunar Poetry   Manifold   Northwords Now
Orbis   Other Poetry   Poetry Monthly
Smiths Knoll   Stride   Tears in the Fence   The Journal
Ver   Wandering Dog

Other books by Grahame Barrasford Young

Ragnarok Reborn — Outposts
Fractures — Brans Head
Lynsongs — Brans Head
Glenfinnan, mostly — Brans Head
Routes of uncertainty — Original Plus

Author photograph: Fiona Gibson
Cover photograph by the author

Table of Contents

Cornish farm, 1972	1
Where	2
Mollycoddling	3
Who grows old, hasn't tried enough	4
Reading-room Regular	5
Response to an Editor's response	6
Now, too late, I ask	7
Twist	8
Ars longa...	9
Fracture	10
Prelude	12
Night and day	13
Vallis Vale	15
Spring Song	16
Dreich	17
The locked gate at Moy	18
Later	20
Lacking empathy	21
Extinction event	22
Interference	23
Orphic	24
Rebirth	25
Hope	26
...and the women calling	27
The unnecessary death of an otter cub in a new hydro scheme	33
Risk	37
The camera never lies	38
Sanctuary	39
Beginning late, finishing later	40
Infinity	41
How should we dare?	42
Thursday's child	43
Descending Schiehallion	44
Inadequacy	45
Neutering wilderness	46
Because I say so	47

Perpetual motion	48
Impermanence	49
The art of moving	50
The engagement of nature and credulity	53
The marriage of landscape and understanding	54
Dream as quantum leakage	56
Even the densest atom is nearly empty	58
Accidental	59
Seeing what isn't there	60
Another country	61
Inhabiting De Chirico	62
Skeletons	63
Revising a Sussex Garden	64
Recircled	65
Early eco	66
Severn unopposed	67
Storm now, rain later	68
The persistence of indifference	69
She has no mouth but she must scream	70
On the supposition that life came to earth from space	71
Beginnings	72
The poetic impulse	73

Cornish farm, 1972

Cutting a calf's head off
involves nothing slick, no modern art
of pretty patterns swirled red through red,
but crushed tubes, blood, tendons hanging.
It means not trudging miles for tools
while a calf suffocates in unburst birth,
her cow in agony, which is poor husbandry,
but having blades to hand:
when animals go wrong
kill the child;
a cow's worth more alive.

But still we took an hour
to excavate its twin, flopped out
by exhausted animals and men,
swung pendulum on a rope:
after all that fight to be alive
it would choke unless we drained its throat,
hoping straight from womb,
hanging, it hadn't learned terror,
bewildered eyes blurring black and white arcs –
after we let her down we almost cheered
when she struggled to her feet.

A few months on, you ate her.

Where

... I peed in an outside drain
strutting grown-up at three,
but cowered in bed
as a giant bull breathing
filled my room with sleeplessness.

... one evening at 8
after a freedom of tricycling our block
my soft sense of self was told
it would be sent back
if it escaped again.

... we sprawled,
our night so slow stars moved,
your dog on its long lead
made sure our warmth
remained external.

... light was sudden on your hair,
you read my words
to show how poor they were
against your being, how little they gave
for what I took.

... understanding sees that these
are inextricable:
without first, no consequence,
but, most clear,
without last no first. ◢

Mollycoddling

Stepped pits, deeper than we were tall,
at the bomb site down the road,
were graves for packing case tanks
liberated from the bottle-cap works.
In Thames sand, they flooded at spring tides.

We must have drowned so many times
in those fox-holes of our war,
broken every arm or leg
escaping through an always sudden
parent-baiting dark.

When my brother nose-dived
from the howdah of a slide
we wiped blood with grass
and the drinking tap,
and didn't take him home till tea.

I only drowned properly
off Broadstairs beach,
sinking twice, age six,
in sight of parents,
a thousand adults watching.

Who grows old, hasn't tried enough

You're still sixteen, says my mind,
and had my early work not been chucked
for lacking far more than rhythm,
might wonder if thought stays that age.

Moments where you move on
are disturbingly nebulous:
choosing a doctor, owning a car;
a key to your own door,
none quite remembered decades later.
There's no answer, just an acceptance
all these moments contribute to a whole
that left its teens perhaps unwillingly.

Some are clearer: when I was eight
I went to the library one evening,
and, with no proper map to walk
between Plato and science fiction
astronomy and Zane Grey, Assyria and art,
beautifully lost, never came back.

Reading-room Regular

When the world thought education
worth paying for a few papers flat-paged
beneath their brass containing rods,
this man read right through,
every day from opening to close.
Marvellous at quizzes, bar philosopher,
he could dazzle each day with facts
you didn't need to know existed.

But there he was, sometimes a little late
from another job he couldn't hold,
because knowing is not knowledge –
and while the world agreed the cost of news,
it wouldn't pay to teach him when to think:
though he'd charm free teas from anyone,
the brass rod holding down his temper
too often came undone ⁄⁄

Response to an Editor's response

"You don't engage with..."
people, a truth,
not dealing because I suffer

    so much so I don't
see a point in explanation –
except, it started early,

quite soon after birth,
and when it most mattered
was reinforced, severely.

I've never found a method
to get undone,
but sometimes I try to say. . .

Others do people
much better, anyway.

Now, too late, I ask

Once eyes bright with love
dismissed me that same night,
and I did not learn to read the signs.
I have watched bodies and mis-read,
mis-read bodies and watched.
Those who cannot read, can't.

Never hugged, never held,
while friends consumed their nights
with diaphanous tricky underwear,
in my teen dreams sexless mannequins
cuddled, soothed and stroked.

My landscapes of unsure desire
baffled by this unkeyed map,
could not connect with trust or love,
until, storm-squashed and seventeen
in an Ealing cemetery shelter,
only Joe's patrolling creaky boots
saved me..
I wish he'd not stopped.

I still cannot read
anything but a book.
Or trust too much.

Twist

I have for a long time
avoided water,
except by boat.

I have for a shorter time
avoided air,
except by nothing.

For even less but overlong a time,
I have avoided connection,
except

this is involuntary,
beginning at the longest time
in my false orphan's bed

before I could learn to cope,
and now I want exception
it will not come. ⁄⁄

Ars longa...

Here, the poet arrogant with art
conducting great music on their room's tv.
There, her, having a hot long bath.

Blood on his thigh next morning
was not passion but the taking from them
of a child he had not wanted.

He grieved briefly, in his own way:
chords that delighted became sharp,
once loved paintings black and white.

When colours came back he looked for good,
but let indifference become a loss of loss.
Soon he returned to his conducting game.

Later, he would suborn art to life,
where some achievement lies
and only return when he found words. ⁄⁄

Fracture

Quartz intrusions in bright granite,
climbing plastic heads,
wait their turn between leaning sky bent cliff,
looking backwards in perpetual homage
down to water, across the valley,
where a shepherd presumes authority,
shuts out reality: 'this land is mine,'
drives us from what owns us.

Brittle bones in a low sun
combine with wild shadows of broken trees
to stretch and stitch the present hills,
thrill the innocent on his safe rock,
imbue the space with age. But not the stone,
whose age each flood diminishes and expands,
down and backwards (as we might move
down and back across sedimentary cliffs),
draining through ammonite coil of groping root
to slicken where water-boatmen whirl.

Escaped towards hills we drop,
to where the high hill silence softens,
bird-song can echo and mellow, fill
hollows we did not expect, strip us
note by note while whirligigs
wild on dead places of the stream
hypnotise, leave us detached,
unreached by sideways
suddenness of leaping spider,
the grab of unsheathed tiger.

We have stood by foaming rivers,
trodden drab corpses of our progress,
on ripped earth, in torn earth,
beneath hills misshapen in the watered sun
that shadows twists and strain,
where only distance alleviates enormity
and man diminishes.

Here, for the moment, we are safe.
Air clean, this water pure.
There are boats on the stream,
sticks from idle hands;
rainbows beneath the cloud; below us
grasses heavy with rainbow snails;
the slow surge of the mountain, breathing.

Curled on grey rock,
you initiate a memory of place.
But not of here, not here.
Here we are too old, and the fires formed us,
and we did not escape, though some did,
to the sea with news and no past.
Were they the fortunate ones,
living the true loneliness of half-recall,
songs with lost melody, blurred faces,
frames without canvas, streets with no home.
This is the true isolation,
their landscape without shadow, stunted,
their plain unstitched in snow.

Which leaves us, with our bird-song,
waterfall, scoured rock, static
in unconcern. Calcified. Ammonites.
Stopped coils on a grey rock.
We in homage to this place
replace those who climb,
who look backwards down the valley
as looming brackens interrupt distance,
constrict grey waters, shut off the sky,
until alone without dreams
we look to ourselves and can only ask;
who are the fortunate ones,
who cannot remember? ⁄⁄

Prelude

Thighs that naked rode moons
rising from Silbury's depth,
on a bank at Osterley parting,
take another moon within their dark.
I watch, ceding your solitary love.
And when, glistening on grass,
you ask what I cannot answer,
our eyes give substance to lost ease,
light of many moons does not disguise,
gave stark contrast where we would hide.

Such reality stretches the long dark home;
we hear owls deride while deaf to speech,
later wonder who did sneer or sadden.
You naked in grass might weep
as words exposed my emptiness,
but unsure of answering sensibly
while sensing end, I might laugh to know
your mantis love could not devour me,
before I wept that it would not.

Night and day

Light draining from hillsides
erodes gullies. Broken glass assumes
the glimmer of fireflies,
flickers, fades. The gift of darkness
drifts over the short grass, settles
round stems of short grass,
seals the cool earth. Scent of closing.
Now, after certain darkness,
some see a risen face of god.
Others the hill's hunch
of loneliness, the clasped knees
secure against cold drifts of dew
turning to pale translucent skin
that masks the short blade, heather frond,
mottles the hillside, stiffens.

Left to consider, night, you home,
moon set. I among strange people
exquisitely spaced beyond reach.
Sodium lights them. Its yellow glooms
their moving lips and hides their mood,
lets them speak too much from shadow
deepened by light. Thus, hearing
'yes' when unseen lips said 'no'
I let you leave from my tight cone.
In blazing midnight my dark revolves
spun by your departing scorn
through crowded artificial streets.
The many win you. In gold-plated oily water
only the symmetry of glass suns reflects.

Gaunt parallelograms of rust
pin to grey sand. Rainbow pools
kill. The sun reflected at dawn
is moon. Sluggish water slops rock.
Define: a light that softens this
cannot be unnatural – 'honeyed',
'damp', 'grey'; descending gloom, all inadequate.
There are no words for light
that will mask reality or mist that gaunt
to you outstretched pinning earth to sky,
Medusa with the head of Perseus
held to your barrenness – or
or are you merely tousled, bare breasted,
beckoning, myself at whim to charm
stranded in the midst of clarity?

Noon now: after certain darkness
this is the risen god, blank, silent,
light of night and evening, dawn,
drawn together, white, total light,
to burn barrenness, dissolve skin
to pain, stretch like old skin on bone
a mind that learnt to cover heart.
Here vigil ends, as sun crests
the ridge and creases it.
Light draining from the sun illuminates:
we can see beyond shadow
for a while. Yet we unready reach
through pain, not for calm shade,
rather for masks to extinguish light,
because like total light,
total knowledge hurts. ◢

Vallis Vale

This is a naming day,
when you tell me, again,
that here is celandine,
there wort. Forgotten names
fill a space between plants
and leave me once more,
so my refreshed delight
is set against your new,
in knowing this scabious
is blue, this yellow, rue. ⁄⁄

Spring Song

Wintered by neglect
your cycle lurks small in grass.
You see a Lilliputian stag:
"Daddy look, the handlebars"

glint across veldt
a pride of household lions
stalk vulture sparrows
until scattered
by sudden coils of python hose
they remember urgent chairs

Stripped by spring heat,
chaining rye grass,
you dissolve, child no more,
a stranger I cannot deny,
yet do so every day.
Sustained by ivy I will uproot,
what future do you hide
among your tropic leaves?

Dreich

This is soaking soft rain,
not that splashy type
bouncing from coats
so hard we don't stay wet
when it has passed.

This is a soaking rain,
that seeps and crawls,
oozes into defences
as if you'd forgotten them.
It burrows through seams
and does not dry
when it moves on.

This is a soaking rain,
drenching and clammy,
that despite its softness
bruises before it stops,
and does not clean.

The locked gate at Moy

At Moy, past its locked gate,
people move.
I could not walk through,
would not climb,
in a place meaning nothing,
in a spot I could have passed,
knowing my foot might catch
in deer-fence wire, become

knucklebones under an open cage;
wind-rolled, meaning nothing,
my skull, dribbled by sheep,
myopic on mica,
ribs whistling to scare birds

This foreseen closes a glimpsed past
where some walked with me
across scree slopes,
above photogenic paths
that lead to Moy,
irredeemably empty.

Without an Adlestrop, Innisfree,
where memory can stop down
to isolate one pleasure from fraught times,
or open full when part might hurt,
with nothing framed to contemplate,
I looked beyond artifice
to where crags gave to commanding ice,
but turn us still.

It is why we come,
thinking to climb forever,
wait beneath auroras as if dead,
pampering our pain,
unreal at midpoints hills impose.

No stations, no islands:
oozes, water unsullied by death,
contours bounding undistinguished rocks,
mere vantages of silence, no use to those
who must always stop for tea.

We walk from people, out of society,
as long as need tells us
solitude will be enough,
that fields dreamt are real,
that we can reap them when we wake.

How safely we escape.
At every pass there is only down:
towards solitude; back through fields
hoping the spoiled film of our journey
can be discarded into storm.

Off the hill, regiments of comfort begin:
desks in their boredom, fruit on fields,
rules of office, rules of home,
everything auroras ease.
We check our maps with these in view,
wonder still which way we should have turned.

It would be the simplest choice
if we did not always come
to a locked gate at Moy.
Beyond it people move.

Later

After the event,
he sat on a step and stared
until someone draped a sheet,
took away that last, ridiculous, hope,
for the first time.

Earlier, and much earlier,
neither he nor she
had fretted enough
to need more than acceptance
that this must happen.

Her heart was too quiet
to be properly heard,
though her life spoke:
kindness should be paramount,
love is too precise.

Lacking empathy

Whose funeral are you closing for? he asks,
steps back twice as, brutally, I tell him,
turns and speechless leaves the shop.

Is there a better way?

When my mother died, the old lady
arriving for her hair appointment
a month on, shrivelled to my 'She died'.

Is there a better way?

These happened to me and are mine:
if I must cope, so must they,
who have no proper tie.

Extinction event

After the first death,
the rest, one by one, shared,
normalised, will be endured.

After earthquake, war, tsunami,
only those who live can feel.
Our response is mere observance.

Family, refugees, half a nation:
how far can grief be stretched
before it becomes indifference?

After the worst death,
I looked for my others,
and could not recover them.

Interference

Looking for the rain I climbed
from drought dry onto arid hill.
Sky greeted me, hot empty, blue
reflecting in scoured quartz.
A thousand feet below, churning dust
mocked lost cloud inversions.

I descended, let the hill guide my feet
until, stumbling, I kicked out a rock.
Water oozed: foolishly I kicked again.
Flood threw me aside. When I stood,
all dust was gone, the glen's detritus
carved into intricate braids
like the map of a life scalpels
scarred into your saved flesh.

Orphic

The dead don't need Hades,
they have nothing to forget:
only their left-overs do.

I went instead, understanding
no one would come for me,
that I would patrol endlessly along Lethe,
afraid to cross, unable to return.

One late day I understood
you had already come for me:
what else could have dragged you
across half a world?

I did not need to stay.

Rebirth

Even when Facebook trends
how can this become habitual,

people with sad ashes blown back
into their faces?

When it was you
we were high on a safe rock,

but half of what was meant for sea
ended disappointingly in grass.

I found a magic cockle shell,
rim rococo-ed by worms.

Inside, a barnacle
imitates Mons Olympus.

It waits on my desk
for a dry Venus to rise.

Earth and water confer
different immortalities.

Hope

Heard you yesterday

did not realise you were words

took significance
to be an intermittent breeze

wondered why breeze
should sound so many things
I would want to hear ⁄⁄

...and the women calling

Our unhung church bell
rung by tourists with a wooden club
no longer urges the devout
or summons our defenders.
Downhill in my writer's chair
I hear it call and call
out of corries and remembered cwms.
How far back,
how far back?
Propped alone, it cannot peal
for victory, queen's accolade or leader's death,
can only in its dull toll
move me where

    arrogant with youth we abandon age,
abdicate futures, seeing no need,
ask too late where we should learn,
in which silences find growth.
We wait the catastrophic crash seen as age
to curtail noise, fade sense's input
long enough to clear a file that takes new code.
    Silence is all we get:
outside walls all erect before solitude
feathers fall in open fields
snowflakes on water, cats walk silk,
stardust sifts to earth.
Their cacophony shatters memory;
icons thought immutable cascade,
reload themselves, scatter intention,
contention overloads capacity.
We search familiarity for ways to isolate
false pasts, impose order from din,
until   one small icon, placed
where it should have always been,
gives entry to that resonance.

Dark against sunrise, one morning
you will walk out of landsbreath,
find me, unfleshed again by time,
eroded from my nest of dead lamb's wool.
If you stop, I might tell stories of great lords,
parliaments of beasts, of running here
to make sleep a virtue.
Only one will be true;
how of things considered, things promised,
things planned, your old age was never one,
how, knowing this, still
our shadows did not embrace enough,
or long, how there are places you so inhabit
I cannot even dream of them.

So here I am, with a blurred horizon
where enfolding stones shiver in a wind
that curves and carves old grass, fresh corn,
sitting to excavate colour lost to chequered youth:
sepia Carcassonne, pale Urbino,
white Communion dresses coning canals,
black of a midnight Via Veneto,
umbrella-ed to Englishness, drunk with red negroni,
white by the Bodensee, expounding rococo to a reeling boy,
no awareness of Spanish Pisa, Dutch Madrid,
where only beer and bars were different,
at Avignon a bridge colourless in night-mist

(outside Warwick's walls your bridge
was green and Babylon, long light speckled
from roistering water heckled comfortable arches
until evening butterflies and dapple and homing birds
swirled in warmth and were ours)

that bar where her breasts in straining white
did not remember yours, nor her legs in black:
leaning to serve another beer
why is her teenage image clearer than your thirty years?
You I did not know

now billow sail, spill me down quicksand
bleached bones dance darkness
dance darkness starred with your vacuum
dance darkness parched bone
white of your hand on great stones
fingers tracing rough stone,
my voice echoing against cool stone

'they used sandstone, weathers quickly
to false age, circumstance, sanctity;
granite, at great cost, polished
lets slide blood beneath this stone they found
a blade obsidian sharp a shaman's knife
to ensure their dancing sacrifice really dies'
you did not believe stone absorbed sense
you moved away I dance darkness
loomed with empty stone
staring at strange shapes of clouds
until we drive into walls and are astonished
by silence I could not cry
darkness dance please dance
she breathes....does not breathe....breathes
martins over evening-still streams are more decisive
broken-backed sheep emptied down rock
are more decisive

apprehension grows spades split earth
move the skull we buried long ago
time and place forgotten unhook her here
open her out free viscera
split throat to thigh for her mute voice
of blood I know little watch it stain
through an artery to her heart
of the matter matter no matter
see her dance
the wench is dead blood for the beggar
no matter the wench is dead
did die and I am gone to chair

Tara, that's for kings;
too late for Cadair, only madness there;
more Devils' than I need, none are needed:
Earth no more talks through stone
than stone is bone of magicked men.
Her voice is where we cannot listen,
huge tablets dipping to renewal
in a fuse of fire and chemistry.
Afterwards she is mute.
Silence returns.

Do you remember trailing your dog
beneath amber leaves, through dead leaves
carelessly flurried by our feet.
Where leaves draped, so did our arms.
I asked then: she refused, praising me

(by Cornish sand trees in spirals
crowded to talk among themselves
while we were young and unconstrained
and walked and sang spring's long swell)

Our trees were bare; through them,
once, by accident, we watched
brief Perseids explode their rage
at long celestial banishment,
burn their firework dust,
ending for our delight in a cherished dream
that gave expectation its myth.
Stay of my mast, flesh of my bone,
chord of my scattered notes
you are dusted into sound and sand,
tasted by fish, recycled for egg-shell,
unseen ever again,
always there when we want to look.

When we stood
as spurned cloud split
to let light spill
across the stone,
imagination gathered
all that radiance
of water, earth, and hidden sky
to make a nimbus
round your memory.
Such an icon,
which should
have burned across skies
instead shifts
endlessly,
your face darkened
by after-images
of your sun.
Will that shadow
darken me
as the sense
of our fables is erased
by my striving
to prove them true.
I need light
cascading through dark hills
before I endure
as dust
outside your wall.

Even dark moons speak each night,
perfume of words, citrus sight.
Time was lilacs grew when they should;
time was, after I followed
footprints still freshly yours
across sands of levelled hills,
tracks loved when snow was deep
on ridges hawks no longer watch,
I would have been dead,
laid east to west as in church,

my nave of glen and altar hills
to satisfy any need of comfort,
stags as my mourners.

Time was, shadow grew apprehensive
memory might skew,
reconstruct what it needed
to fix those transient moments,
project perfection on one
ordinarily human.
Time was lilacs would have been so cruel,
but they grew from sucker to tree

and that is time enough to grow
from emptied hull to full-rigged ship,
pass childhood's stages with more knowledge,
a little less pain, until teen absurdity –
emptiness of waiting, butterflies
amok at every half-heard radio ring,
words that stumble before they're out,
lets me claim that like youth
love is wasted on the young,
bringing certainty of voice,
certainty of place, smile,
certainty of hand, touch,
certainty all golden treasures,
that vase, this bowl, are not worth
a single one of these
without you to share.

Dust reforms:
it is not you,
it cannot be you,
it should not be you,
but must in part be you,
because each brings to me
something always lacked,
and that has not changed.

The unnecessary death of an otter cub in a new hydro scheme

Dark hydro water turbines back to light
behind my house.
At its high intake a cub caught
in unnatural rock

       fights

            concrete scours her cubsilk pelt

       concrete strips her skin to gut

her bones break   her will fails

in wild trapped water
that should have buoyed her
she fought

and did she not feel terror
at that slow closing of body,
fear the dark claws
fingering through her eyes?

She did not know of death,
but felt something fail
and found no gentleness.

Not being aware of extinction
makes it no easier.

Risk

One who walked on eggs
said: hard this,
perhaps not useful,
worth a try;

hope springing
is spoilt by fear:
a wind-shut door
is not reopened,

though it kills
any counterpoint of falls,
late evening paths
dappling waves. ⁄⁄

The camera never lies

Turning landscape
black and white
(cliffs not lost
in tumble-death green,
heather-mottle
polka-dotting snow)
makes it easier
to see the anomaly:
a raven practising take-off
to impress its mate
giving unexpected balance
to a blur against rock
that is your face

– if that is your face,
how can there be no colour?
If that is your face
why are you so far?

Sanctuary

Never been there when you are,
the small secret place to which
now and then there is a way.

Never there when you might solve
problems that grow between trips,
ones you could quickly answer
should we ever share that space.

Somehow though we do not meet,
and when we do, in real time,
such things are never said. ⧸⧸

Beginning late, finishing later

Thirty years, or more: a year of light
(some days of night) to get this far.

Walking in, walking out, never time enough
down the slices of the ridges' fetch.

These hills are brown, or bright with winter.
From where I look, distant ranges

I might not walk are insubstantial,
never pale or blue. All that is real

is the sea-washed summit pebble
I found for you. ◢

Infinity

When winds co-operate, it seems
goldie and buzzard, looping back
through the patterns of their slow rise
really could fly forever, watching,
while we on the ground flick
through our unswerving lives. ⁄⁄

How should we dare?

A long climb over brittle rock.
A mid-point lost in weather.

We stop to brew, chocolate bars,
still but for out drinking hands,
companionably quiet.

Mist oozes round us.
Six feet left, cloud eddies,
twin suns appear.

Excitedly alerting you,
I bruise your ribs.

Briefly perplexed,
golden eyes consider, dismiss,
amused by pour presumption.

Feathers flex in a shiver of mist.

Wings spread nearly to touch,
a god slides out of reach.
Whorled droplets caress it
as we follow it out of sight.

It takes spirit with it,
leaves awe.
Forever distant
we are inextricably linked
through our unswerving lives.

Thursday's child

Why are you looking down?
Two, three, hours ago you walked there,
recognised asphodel and cotton grass, wild violets.
By the hissing grumble of narrowed spate
you kicked scat and spraint,
crumbled a tawny's pellet to find
a tiny skull and meagre bones,
watched scuts bounce across a knoll.

You're here now, above a swathe of flattened colour
you don't quite remember walking,
though all too aware of the effort
moving from that crag to this –
a finger's width on the map,
a long haul through snow so gritty
it seems like a whirl of papers heavy with words,
sent to waste, returned shredded by an unkind wind.

Don't look down.

Descending Schiehallion

Where peace begins,

down from the slice and din
of frozen gale, stumbling
never-to-be-trusted drift,
as tumbled ptarmigan flirt with us,
a dance troupe off their beat,
that last mile of slither,

all movement briefly stops.

Amber-shackled by late sun
a still hawk haunts dusk.

Inadequacy

Read for me
in the voice
that fills silence.

My words
must come back
from the one
who fills silence.

Take my words
and offer them:
let me hear
how poor they are
against your being

how little they give
for what I take.

Neutering wilderness

When men took nothing to the hill
but necessary gear,
reaching corries where plucked rock
shreds noise and folds it into cracks

(so once they rested all they'd hear was blood
flowing through their ears)
did they complain incessantly about the quiet?

Now that age tries to defend me from the hills,
I want to know which sounds excited you
when you left the corrie's mouth –

the bass and kettle drum of melt over rock and stone?
A jay's broken bassoon? Ptarmigans' punctured horn?
A breeze orchestrated through closed and open trees
until its blood-red lingering drew you deep?

Or perhaps only the pebble-pianos'
abrupt abdication of their future,
dissipating in a devil's trill of washed-out green?

But you choose to listen to a plastic sing-along.
In silence or nature, what are you so afraid to hear? ⫽

Because I say so

I have clustered my meanings
into lines, tied them tight,

to stay together when you thrust
a critical knife – and yet

allowed movement enough
to let you take what you want.

I will not read them to you:
if you hear my voice,

you can never avoid
what I thought I meant. ⁄⁄

Perpetual motion

On our track under snow,
time spreads:
my marker tree,
where I spoke to a fox,
must have been a mile ago,
yet space between eagles' rock,
that tree where buzzards rest,
expands,
until,
knowing precisely otherwise,
our path looping
quark-like, mind decides
both have been passed
but never reached.

Only unbroken snow
says it is not so.

Impermanence

Days on our bicycles,
drinking and racing
(wrong way round, you'd think)
climbed hills to beat cars down:
one left, and another came,
it was not the same.

Days at the library chute,
1000 recycles every night,
singing and joking to readers
through our intercom:
one left, and another came,
it was not the same.

Days on your rusty Vespa,
down and up to the coast,
stealing beds, sharing cuisine,
wet feet under a yellow cape:
one left, and another came,
it was not the same.

Days when I cultivate my land
with trees and shrubs and moss,
rich with slow-worm and newt,
small birds, fruit, bright beetles:
I will leave, and another come,
it will not be the same.

The art of moving

With no place to come from, life has moved me,
from capital to town to village, always wondering
if this might be the Belong. I have never been sure.

Instead there is the Always hill, where rock, grass,
reed, bog, a view of lochs and faint ranges,
cannot be other than what I think it is.

In my time, rock, frosted and baked, has flaked,
miniscule deaths changing little, but atom by atom,
speck and speck, seed by seed, all has been made soil.

It has dried, soaked, dried, into blown dust:
will I become part of its slow consolidation,
(easy in a world that prefers to burn), or follow

a dream, a wish: lovers on a quiet slope, leaning on rocks
that allow landscape, covered by bracken to warm their
bodies
as dead lips touch, intimately belonging,

trees sprout from flesh, small scurrying things grow fat,
the parts not feasted by hawk and beetle become moss,
bones mix with chitin and antler, into dust.

It would be lonelier than any tryst,
but not alone while the multitude swarms
towards what death has offered.

It would be hidden, so there can be no music,
no mournful Bruch, no last Strauss.
Just eagles calling on the wind. Enough.

The engagement of nature and credulity

Cumulus you would not dare dream
spills like Jovian storms
in whorls and empty violent eyes,
endlessly over apprehensive peaks
that have not known such June stupidity.
Smoke clouds above flash-fired gorse,
brushes grey across the flattened grass,
strobes rock to unexpected dance.

Under such skies, light stutters.
Gates appear which once were gorges.
From this cloud, this drift – this rare –
anything might come; overwhelming,
making drab of hillside dragonflies,
an exultation that covers all in shade,
scorches detail, obscures the old,
cannot illuminate the new.

Sensing novelty, the weary congregate,
move forward, posture, preen, pronounce,
then directionless, uncertain, still.
Coveted newness needs no revelation,
but words are all they know, so words are sought
like glow-worms in a boulder-field,
that could never guide through night.

Disconsolate in groups,
some debate smoke, some cloud,
others beg insects for more light.
All watch for midnight sun to set,
anxious that shadows cast so long
will confuse them when they turn.

And they do turn, and turn again,
into themselves, against themselves,
our interest, until gates revert
and there is no way in. ⧫

The marriage of landscape and understanding

Suddenly the track

Hold on! If this is the track from last week, last year,
smothered in common spoor, struggling with its Moebius knot,
shouldn't there be resolution, miles mused distilled?
There must be more this time than another hoofprint,
sheep strung, Christmas lights, down evening slopes,
grass cobbled with basking deer.

Behind locked gates, lost in uncertain's slurries,
Some endlessly refresh their pain
through borrowed sorrow, do not ease their own;
    explain, unless others speak
none exist, however linked they try to be;
    find only movement excites,
obscuring memory, refusing flesh.
All lured in dream, running lost
where truth or falsehood trap,
not knowing which is function, which cure,
with no escape unless one moves
and if one moves no escape.

suddenly the track,
no more a path that goes
where it comes back from,
loses perspective,
broadens distantly out of trees,
to lift across cliffs towards Pluto,
flirt with suns, bypass starfields,
tunnel dark matter, overtake
fleeing galaxies, redshift invisible.

Move forward then, bored by stasis,
exult in ambiguity –

wave-jumping bare boys turn to girls;
lyric drought to silent flood;
new stars die first, the brightest are black.
Take indecision, prism, spin white;
when loved voices are mute
do not fret – you know
that where love takes us after such a start
can never be finite when it allows
all universes in which to challenge pain.

If this is last week's, year's, youth's, track,
walked steadily, it has yet to double back. ⫽

Dream as quantum leakage

Here's a reality:
we make our choices, you and me, this or that,
and every time divide, each offshoot
to begin a different life, a different life
that never starts with question one,
until we move too far from here to recognise,
and everything we forgot to do, or wanted to,
or could not conceive, is done.

Here's a reality:
from town through chalkwater fields
down hard drops this erosion never made –
a pebble that didn't move, a storm that passed –
their scarps to noisy sea climbing
hopscotch through volcanic butterflies that fly
through shattered factories where
a scoop of clean water is worth death

Are these my lives, our lives,
dreamed, recurring, moving on,
people changing: conversation continued
as I walk with others, drink with others,
build with others, none I have known?
Is this a dreamland peopled with unseens,
resurrecting something utterly forgotten:
factory, farm, great volcanic hill –
as if!
       or
              These are my lives,
so many fissions off – 100 or a trillion? –
none close enough to be inevitable,
each unavoidable, parallels spreading.
While decoherance is paralysed by sleep,
allowing no interference from this now,
folded space is opened out,
presenting time to live a strand

where broken shell, footpath, person,
gardens unknown, mysterious countryside,
a house we will one day own,
are variants from every 'yes' or 'no',
places where we turned back or didn't go at all.,
a travelling we can never know.

Here is reality:
that this man a universe of splits aside
might do it differently, his prologue changed,
does not dissolve good –
does not mean a man here,
perhaps already sideways from other selves,
can do wrong because one we cannot meet
will somewhere do it right. ⁄⁄

Even the densest atom is nearly empty

Pointillist poetry's problem:
knowing how many lines
it takes to completely mix a hue,
how many blanks must be filled,
whether anyone will see a whole.

It is not my style, either here
or in life, to overplay colour,
which is not to say I am drab,
just that grey is grey, and that does
– much else overwhelms expectation –
merely that such nuances escape my eyes,
or, at best, my eyes do not transmit
in a way any artist would recognise.

There's my real dilemma:
if a line of walkers is really trees,
or bare remnants of bush
a bag in a most unlikely place,
how should I expect you,
my reader, with your particular vision,
to understand – if this is too dense
it might be better on a museum wall
explaining what words are for,
too simplistic it becomes impression:
really what you're left looking for
are those spaces still between poems.

Accidental

People who knew what they did
have fallen here: are you sure
you need to taunt death,
as if arriving held no danger –
slipping into ravines is a problem
rather like falling down stairs,
though with more excuse,
and often ending less badly.

People who knew what they do
pitch themselves at snow and ice,
and sometimes the fault is not snow's:
however careful, bad luck is bad luck
and you might as well ride the good
until it's either too late,
or you find idle coffee-spoons
a sufficient mark of time.

*

Reference above: I'm up here now,
ambling over snowfields and ice,
bum-bag with waterproof
and chocolate bar, my map,
so though I've paid my dues
I'm bureaucratically illegal,
being alone, half-equipped.

The group struggling down,
smothered in winter gear,
carrying, in a place of springs,
water to restore over-dressed sweat,
tut and glance censorially.
I see them, as I scuff cheerfully on,
follow my footmarks to the glen.

Seeing what isn't there

Forty years since I was here.
They have built, too much perhaps,
still not enough to make it modern.
I see no change.
A South Bank terrace
that was half as wide, at least,
watches Gherkin, Shard, Eye.
I see no change.
On the Tube: at each station
pseudopods of citizens,
hurried, harried,
rush the same pavements, crossings, doors.
I see no change.

Later, Carnac
does not impress with travelogue familiarity,
where youthful unseen Stonehenge,
Forum, Alp, inspired and chilled.
I wonder if memory refuses to see,
release what it thinks it knows,
or diminished by too much information,
we see nothing with our own eyes?
How can we ever be surprised?

Another country

If there were always roads
leading somewhere good,
cut by age's motorway,
what happens on the side we lose?

Did everything stop the day
all synapse bridges broke
decayed and worn, rubble
irretrievable beneath time's tar?

Does unravelling rusted dna
wrap struts already undermined
by corroding drainage pipes,
acids splashed by passing life?

Or do neuron underpasses
redirect and reconstruct,
but need a sense of mischief
to properly explore?

Inhabiting De Chirico

If I wait beneath mountains,
watching, doing nothing because knowing nothing,
there is no hope that things will move themselves
before darkness crooks against the plain.

If I walk the precipice and watch the sky,
while my shadow lengthens in knowledge of the sun,
perhaps squares of darkness will soften into light,
faceless masks grow maskless faces,
stone people warm to life.

Perspectives alter. The stairway weakens.
The tower throws out its dead.
Yet at this edge I want no stairs.
If I descend to the shadow-cubed plain,
on a dark hill I shall be kissed.

Skeletons

He, critic, rightly wants to impale me
if I dwell on oiled old spades and sticky jars,
so there are no grandparents here –
mostly because I only knew one
and 'knowing' is relative, each aware
who the other was, but barely more,
and even now I can't quite like my parents,
who, not being mine, aren't relative,
and uncles (apparently no aunts existed)
never heard of before always appeared
from cupboards where they were kept
for a funeral or a wedding
or a bit of paint-work needing done.
Not a close-knit family, then,
and sadly, now I'm a granddad
I seem to have my own cupboard
out of which I do not come.

Revising a Sussex Garden
(after Samuel Palmer)

Only the noise of servants in the hall
disturbs the lady in her white gown,
as she wafts through flower gardens
beneath a parasol, under a bright sun
that casts long shadows on the barn wall,
passing time to nightfall.

Lady, that light shifted,
pierced bodice, breasts, to bone.
Whiter than your gentle skin
your remnants lay,
charred walls shadow them.

Recircled

Many times I touched those stones
you claim thrill your fingers,
proving earth speaks, has soul.
I'd dismiss you as a fool,
if my ancient bowl had not tingled me
– though this, if real, I'd say
was hand to hand, not rock to flesh.
So, yes, rods I could not control
rolled crossing into the Cove,
and when I strode thrice
widdershins round Avebury
I felt more than endorphins –
but expectation and anticipation
do not make good science,
more an extension of fancy
that need not be recovered.
I cannot repeat that time,
nor would I want to:
erratics, cliffs, strata and crags,
clocks of fire, age and ice,
are so much more relevant
than any failed attempt
to stitch ourselves to heaven.

Early eco

With childhood dams,
it was not impounded water
interested me, but plaits incised
by overflow into sand.

Pleased how a careful finger
shifted braid across braid,
until a twining world
shiny with geology
sifted from earthwork,
I was amazed complexity
would not be simplified
without rock-bomb aid.

On a good day many Amazons
might drain a beach,
until uncaring talkers
with uninterested feet
killed my tides work
as easily as now
they kill a future. ▨

Severn unopposed

When flood,
dangerously deep,
flattens at its peak,
sucks down debris,
imitates a placid lake,
bridges, stranded
in a way no builder
could expect,
become gates:

orb, almond, square,
each to futures
not allowed for:
cackle of loons,
whispers in rotted trees,
weeds through tar,
unloosed dreams.

Trapped by ripples,
their stones drown.

Storm now, rain later

Hard storm kicking
scars, chokes, scours,
mudslips dream to sludge:
stenched cities, unstrung bridges,
strewn dams, mered seas,
ice myth, information smoke.

Who foretold this when fire was made,
wheels broke burden, farms famine,
would be called fool to muse so dark.

So who was fool: we are dispersed,
reduced, left unwhole, creeping
from field to field, to eat remains.

Now this is not a bruising rain;
it sifts over hills, pleasures brooks,
chirrups fledglings at first bath.
Stars have birthed since melt: have we –
enough to keep some hold on life
while Earth renews hope.

The persistence of indifference
in the face of catastrophe

8000 metres: some climb,
Kraken swim, most wander.

air-weight, water-crush;
interface, so little space in which to live.

Heat unleashed by sudden melt
– crawls high;
swifts die of air, cloud diverts,
winds haphazard,
sun waters

– crawls deep;
fish die of flood, plankton stultify,
food chains unravel,
ocean stinks

– crawls north;
dust deep as herons
chokes fawn, fox, farm,
peacocks Pole

– crawls south;
swallows dead of drought,
rivers suck ocean back to source,
salts starve.

8000 metres: some slide,
Kraken feed, most flounder.

One interface, expanding shut. ⁄⁄

She has no mouth but she must scream

if her lungs were still
our breathing would be laboured;

if her tears were not shed
our bodies would be withered;

if her ears heard only what she knew
our silence would be absolute;

if her bones were never broken
our soil would stay infertile;

if her green dress was all she wore
our boredom would be deadly;

if her eyes reflected only dark skies
our horizons would be too narrow;

if her blood had not been shed
our lives may not have happened;

when she at last explodes her pain
how can we ignore 'enough'?

On the supposition that life came to earth from space

some say   *this* sun can't birth
but *others* can, spurting life about,
through utter outerness
sillyseconds into universe

atoms clump, reform,
galaxy sun child
with odds so huge
a shiver fluttering
not shivering
would end us
   before

no sense
why flare as seed, nova,
haystack galactic, planet needle,
infinite coconuts, one shy.
Is this fear
that they don't know if
it takes a billion years,
a billion seconds or one
for stew to mix, procreate.
and are afraid
that life is not unique

     or because it is? ⧄

Beginnings

Eight swallows wavering on wires
quaver the Fifth against cloud
when I wander from my trees.

All that's left, such accident?

– only so many muses for one life;
wine too soon stops what it starts;
poverty only available to the poor;
divine ecstasy no longer fuses,
coke-fuelled hell is not a threat.
A bit of smoulder, no flair –

Bring on decline – except

Eight swallows
two-finger decline far into touch,
six-hit it out of stadiums:
dropped by startled passers-by,
it breaks. ⁄⁄

The poetic impulse

In its proper season,
at a precise moment of tide,
Wye does not mix with Severn,
laking bright hill water
against meadows' brown –
until, one atom moving,
it all collapses into sea. ▰

Other anthologies and collections available from Stairwell Books

Awakening	Richard Harries
Geography Is Irrelevant	Ed. Rose Drew and Amina Alyal, Raef Boylan
Belong	Ed. Verity Glendenning and Stephanie Venn, Amy E Creighton
Out of the Dreaming Dark	F.Mary Callan and Joy Simpson
A Stray Dog, Following	Greg Quiery
Blue Saxophone	Rosemary Palmeira
Waiting at the Temporary Traffic Lights	Graham Lee
Steel Tipped Snowflakes 1	Izzy Rhiannon Jones, Becca Miles, Laura Voivodeship
Where the Hares Are	John Gilham
Something I Need to Tell You	William Thirsk-Gaskill
The Glass King	Gary Allen
The River Was a God	David Lee Morgan
A Thing of Beauty Is a Joy Forever	Don Walls
Gooseberries	Val Horner
Poetry for the Newly Single 40 Something	Maria Stephenson
Northern Lights	Harry Gallagher
Nothing Is Meant to be Broken	Mark Connors
Heading for the Hills	Gillian Byrom-Smith
More Exhibitionism	Ed. Glen Taylor
Rhinoceros	Daniel Richardson
The Beggars of York	Don Walls
Lodestone	Hannah Stone
Unsettled Accounts	Tony Lucas
Learning to Breathe	John Gilham
The Problem with Beauty	Tanya Nightingale
Throwing Mother in the Skip	William Thirsk-Gaskill
New Crops from Old Fields	Ed. Oz Hardwick
The Ordinariness of Parrots	Amina Alyal
Homeless	Ed. Ross Raisin
49	Paul Lingaard
Sometimes I Fly	Tim Goldthorpe
Somewhere Else	Don Walls
Still Life with Wine and Cheese	Ed. Rose Drew and Alan Gillott
Skydive	Andrew Brown
Taking the Long Way Home	Steve Nash
York in Poetry Artwork and Photographs	Ed. John Coopey and Sally Guthrie
Pressed by Unseen Feet	Ed. Rose Drew and Alan Gillott
Scenes from the Seedy Underbelly of Suburbia	Jackie Simmons
Late Flowering	Michael Hildred

For further information please contact rose@stairwellbooks.com
www.stairwellbooks.co.uk
@stairwellbooks